EDWIN MORGAN is one of the foremost Scottish poets of the twentieth century. He was born in Glasgow in 1920 and grew up in Rutherglen. His studies at Glasgow University were interrupted in 1940 when he joined the Royal Army Medical Corps, but he returned to university and graduated with a First Class Honours degree. Turning down a scholarship at Oxford, he lectured at Glasgow University until his retirement in 1980.

He has published numerous volumes of poetry, and translated works from many languages. His prolific output, as eclectic as it is cosmopolitan, includes *Collected Poems* (1990), *Collected Translations* (1996), *New Selected Poems* (2000), *Cathures* (2002) and *A Book of Lives* (2007); as well as works of criticism and theatre versions of *Cyrano de Bergerac* and *Phèdre*.

His various awards include the Queen's Gold Medal for Poetry in 2000 and the prestigious Weidenfeld Prize for Translation in 2001. From 1999 to 2002 he was Glasgow's first Poet Laureate, and in 2004 was appointed Scotland's first National Poet.

LESLEY DUNCAN is a journalist who studied at Glasgow University (where inspirational lecturers included Edwin Morgan) and Pennsylvania State University, USA. As poetry editor of *The Herald* she chooses the paper's daily poem and also contributes occasional poems herself. She jointly edited *The Edinburgh Book of Twentieth-Century Scottish Poetry* (Edinburgh University Press, 2005) and *The Wallace Muse* (Luath Press, 2005).

ALAN RIACH holds the Chair of Scottish Literature at Glasgow University, is the general editor of the *Collected Works* of Hugh MacDiarmid and the author of *Representing Scotland in Literature, Popular Culture and Iconography* (Palgrave Macmillan, 2005). His fourth book of poems, *Clearances* (2001), follows *First & Last Songs* (1995), *An Open Return* (1991) and *This Folding Map* (1990). His radio series, The Good of the Arts, first broadcast in New Zealand in 2001, may be visited at www.southwest.org.nz

LIZ LOCHHEAD has been Glasgow's Poet Laureate since 2005. She was educated at Glasgow School of Art. Among her collections of poetry are *Dreaming Frankenstein* (1983) and *The Colour of Black & White* (2003). Her stage plays include *Blood and Ice*, *Mary Queen of Scots Got Her Head Chopped Off*, *Perfect Days*, adaptations of *Tartuffe* and (from *Le Misanthrope) Miserygut*, *Medea* and *Thebans*.

Beyond The Sun

Scotland's Favourite Paintings

Poems by
Edwin Morgan
NATIONAL POET OF SCOTLAND

Introduced by
Lesley Duncan
POETRY EDITOR, THE HERALD
and
Alan Riach
HEAD OF SCOTTISH LITERATURE,
UNIVERSITY OF GLASGOW

Afterword by
Liz Lochhead
POET LAUREATE OF GLASGOW

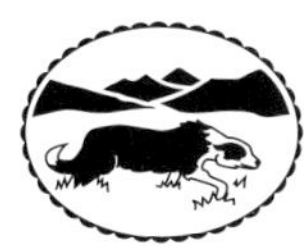

Luath Press Limited
EDINBURGH
www.luath.co.uk

Edwin Morgan, 'To Joan Eardley' from *Collected Poems* (Carcanet Press, 1996), reprinted by permission of the publisher.

Sir Henry Raeburn, *The Reverend Robert Walker Skating on Duddingston Loch* © National Gallery of Scotland.

Salvador Dalí, *Christ of St John of the Cross* © Glasgow City Council (Museums).

F.C.B. Cadell, *The Orange Blind* © Cadell Estate, courtesy of Portland Gallery, London.

Avril Paton, *Windows in the West* © Avril Paton.

El Greco, *Lady in a Fur Wrap* © Glasgow City Council (Museums).

James McIntosh Patrick, *The Tay Bridge from my Studio Window* © McManus Galleries, Dundee City Council.

Jean-Simeon Chardin, *Lady Taking Tea* © Hunterian Museum and Art Gallery, University of Glasgow.

Rembrandt, *Man in Armour* © Glasgow City Council (Museums).

J.S. Sargent, *Lady Agnew of Lochnaw* © National Gallery of Scotland.

Joan Eardley, *Flood Tide* © the estate of Joan Eardley. In the collection of Lillie Art Gallery, East Dunbartonshire Council.

First published 2007

ISBN (10) : 1-905222-72-6
ISBN (13) : 978-1-905222-72-8

The paper used in this book is recyclable. It is made from low chlorine pulps produced in a low energy, low emission manner from renewable forests.

Printed and bound by Scotprint, Haddington

Designed by Tom Bee

Typeset in 12pt Quadraat and Bodoni by 3btype.com

Contents

THE GALLERIES: WHERE TO FIND THE PAINTINGS

Glasgow

Kelvingrove Art Gallery and Museum

Christ of St John of the Cross (1951), Salvador Dalí

The Orange Blind (c.1927), Francis Campbell Boileau Cadell

Man in Armour (1655), Rembrandt

Windows in the West (1993), Avril Paton

Hunterian Art Gallery, Glasgow University

Lady Taking Tea (1735), Jean-Simeon Chardin

Pollok House

Lady in a Fur Wrap (1577–80), El Greco

Milngavie, near Glasgow

Lillie Art Gallery

Flood Tide (c.1962), Joan Eardley

Dundee

McManus Galleries and Museums

The Tay Bridge from my Studio Window (1948), James McIntosh Patrick

Edinburgh

National Gallery of Scotland

The Reverend Robert Walker Skating on Duddingston Loch (1784), Sir Henry Raeburn

Lady Agnew of Lochnaw (1892–3), John Singer Sargent

SCOTLAND'S FAVOURITE PAINTINGS: THE HERALD AND EDWIN MORGAN

The Background Story to Edwin Morgan's Ten Poems on Ten Favourite Paintings in Scottish Public Collections

EARLY IN SEPTEMBER 2005 I found a handwritten envelope among my office mail. 'Dear Lesley,' said the letter inside, 'I seem to be in prolific mood, and send you ten poems inspired by the ten pictures of your competition. They are yours if you find any interest in printing them.' The writer was Edwin Morgan, Scotland's poet laureate. The pictures to which he referred comprised the short leet of a poll of *Herald* readers to find Scotland's most popular painting in a public collection. As the recipient, on behalf of my newspaper, of Professor Morgan's creative largesse, I was not so much interested as thrilled.

My paper's painting poll had been prompted by a joint exercise by the National Gallery in London and Radio 4 to find Britain's greatest picture. It was thought by *The Herald* that purely Scottish paintings would tend to be overlooked in this UK survey (and indeed the only Scottish picture to reach the national shortlist was Raeburn's iconic image of *The Reverend Robert Walker Skating on Duddingston Loch*, ironically itself then at the centre of a dispute over attribution).

The Herald decided to conduct a survey of its own, enlisting the views of various notables in the Scottish arts world, from Richard Demarco to Sir Timothy Clifford. A possible contending picture was featured daily in the paper.

Not surprisingly, the survey attracted much reader interest. Though a small country, Scotland has produced its share of world-class painters, and boasts no fewer than four flourishing art colleges and strong municipal collections (Glasgow's being pre-eminent), as well as the splendid holdings of the National Galleries of Scotland.

The results of *The Herald* survey were announced on 30 August 2005, a week before Turner's *Fighting Temeraire* emerged as the rather unlikely UK winner. The winner of *The Herald*'s poll was altogether more predictable. It was Salvador Dalí's mysterious, beautiful and controversial *Christ of St John of the Cross*, from Glasgow's own collection. This painting, bought for the city by Dr Tom Honeyman in 1951 for £8,200, a princely sum in the time of post-war austerity, was instantly taken to the hearts of Glaswegians and has continued to be viewed by successive generations of citizens with fierce proprietorial pride.

The Dalí won 29 per cent of readers' votes; *Windows in the West* by Avril Paton 18 per cent; *Flood Tide* by Joan Eardley 11 per cent; *The Orange Blind* by F.C.B. Cadell 8 per cent; The *Tay Bridge from my Studio Window* by James McIntosh Patrick 7 per cent; *Lady Taking Tea* by Jean-Simeon Chardin 7 per cent; *The Reverend Robert Walker Skating on Duddingston Loch*, long attributed to Sir Henry Raeburn, 6 per cent; *Man in Armour* by Rembrandt 6 per cent; *Lady Agnew of Lochnaw* by J.S. Sargent 5 per cent; and *Lady in a Fur Wrap* by El Greco 3 per cent. These choices may not represent cutting-edge modern art (morals could be drawn about public taste on another occasion) but the eclectic, mainstream mix combines the local, national and international in a nicely balanced way and indeed, if percentages are the criterion, the international players make up half the votes.

Meantime, the summer of 2005 was already proving a fruitful one creatively for Edwin Morgan. The 85-year-old poet, though not in good health, had responded instantly to my invitation to write a poem about

William Wallace for *The Wallace Muse*, an anthology of poetry and artwork to mark the 700th anniversary of the Scottish patriot's death. Morgan himself was surprised by the strength of his reaction to Wallace's heroic story and ghastly end.

His poem, *Lines for Wallace*, made an instant impact after its publication in *The Herald*. It was read at the Edinburgh International Book Festival, Stirling Castle, and the Scottish Parliament building in quick succession, and commanded a whole page of the London *Times*.

Now Scotland's national poet was engaging with another part of the nation's heritage, its art collections. This was altogether natural, since Professor Morgan was a discerning art collector and gave his collection to Glasgow University's Hunterian Museum and Art Gallery when he left his West End flat to move into a nursing home.

The ten poems, in his own neat hand (his ancient typewriter having given up the ghost), are fresh and engaging, insightful and witty. They show the poet in top form.

He starts off with the Raeburn, a small picture that packs a big punch. It has acted as an advert for the National Galleries of Scotland both in the UK and internationally (hence its appearance on the British shortlist). Professor Morgan's poem makes no reference to the tenuous claim that it may have been painted by the French émigré Henri-Pierre Danloux. Nor does he dwell on the chilly verisimilitude of the scrolled ice. Rather he responds to the cockiness of the ministerial figure. Pride before a fall is the moral but the image of the drookit reverend happed in his wife's 'mocking shawl' is comic rather than unkind.

Salvador Dalí's painting is an altogether more serious subject, and is treated so by the poet. Doubts have been cast on the genuineness of the painter's Christian fervour (was it a tactical religiosity from a Franco supporter?) but an artist's intentions are in any case irrelevant to how his work communicates with its audience. And its numerous admirers have found both spiritual and aesthetic sustenance in this world-famous painting. Morgan's poem captures the juxtaposition of transcendental and commonplace in the sky-suspended Christ figure and the uninvolved fishermen below. It comments, too, on the curious lack of overt suffering in the crucified god man – 'What happened to the thorns and blood and sweat?'

The Orange Blind by the Scottish Colourist F.C.B. Cadell represents one of the most popular strands of twentieth-century Scottish art. Morgan invokes a playful observer whose orange trains of thought encompass Nell Gwynn and, rather startlingly, West African baboons.

Morgan's response to Avril Paton's *Windows in the West* – the much admired depiction of a disembodied sandstone Glasgow tenement – produces one of the most imaginative pieces in the cycle. He first sees the building as a creature in its own right before offering kaleidoscopic fragments of the great variety of human life and condition seething away under its roof. The life and strife it contains could outdo *Anna Karenina* and *The Great Gatsby*, he suggests, before ending on a note of gentle bathos: 'Coffee up.' / 'My God another cracked cup'.

El Greco's anonymous *Lady in a Fur Wrap* maintains her aloofness and mystery in Morgan's eyes:

Whoever she was,
She gives the world an unforgettable glance
From which we don't advance
With names.

Back in the world of contemporary Scotland, James McIntosh Patrick's *The Tay Bridge from my Studio Window* not only takes as its subject one of the country's great Victorian engineering projects but allows Morgan to explore the artistic vision and technique behind what seems at first glance an almost photographic depiction. This is genuine, sympathetic, art criticism from Morgan and is all the more cogent for being compressed into a poetic form. He ends with a mischievous reference back to Cadell's orange blind.

Chardin's *Lady Taking Tea* charms Morgan with the power of its sheer ordinariness and simplicity, shunning the grandiloquence of big religious subjects; 'great art can be / An ordinary woman sipping tea', he concludes.

Rembrandt's *Man in Armour*, one of the most prized paintings in the Glasgow collection, fails to rouse Morgan to the expected enthusiasm. The sheer aesthetic beauty of the profiled head and the masterful depiction of the helmet leave him cold. He sees the sitter as a poseur: 'This is a man who has put on some armour / In the cause of art.' That might not seem the ultimate criticism to everybody but Morgan goes on to harangue Rembrandt to return to his real world: 'Bring back your son, yourself, the woman at her bath, / And we'll use words like masterpiece again.'

Is he being deliberately provocative in his following line: 'A cupboard is the best place for jingle-jangle'? The poet certainly shows his critical claws in this piece, though he does end on a more conciliatory note: 'You are great; even a loss from you's a gain. / But do not trivialize the death of men.'

J.S. Sargent's handsome society portrait, *Lady Agnew of Lochnaw*, elicits a two-pronged response from Morgan. First he comments on how the painting shows 'The nature of an aristocracy / That has not gone to seed.' Then he imagines a conversation between sitter and artist, the former begging the latter to make her glamorous. 'But you are glamorous', the painter smoothly retorts before moving to playful admonition:

> But if you had such a splendid nose
> You wanted it more than life size, or wanted two,
> I'd have to pass you over to Picasso.

The imagined Sargent continues with brio:

> Come on now, we are what we are,
> Society painter, society sitter.
> Scrub thoughts of Cleopatra on her litter.

This is not only witty but tackles the limitations of commissioned portraiture, with its implicit expectations of flattery.

Morgan's favourite painting of the ten is Joan Eardley's *Flood Tide*. He has been a long-term admirer of the artist whose work spans the harsh realism of working-class Glasgow and the timeless shore-scapes of the east coast. There's a nod to 'the wild shy boys / She sketched in the city' but the poem is basically a celebration of Eardley, the free creative spirit, as she strides into the salty bluster of a cliff-top in her paint-splashed corduroys.

As she paints, grasses and wild flowers stick to the canvas they've been blown against by the mighty Catterline wind. 'All becomes art.' There's humour, too, in the final solitary clover that is unable to read 'WET PAINT' and is finally fixed to the canvas as:

Part of a field more human than the one
That took the gale and is now
As she is, beyond the sun.

Though their disciplines are different, this is one major Scottish artist's tribute to another.

The ten poems with their accompanying images were first published in *The Herald* on 9 September 2005.

Lesley Duncan
POETRY EDITOR, *The Herald*

POETRY AND PAINTING: SKETCHES FOR AN ESSAY

THE RELATION BETWEEN POETRY and painting is ancient, immediate and vivid, when you think about the ideas behind words like *the line*, *the image*, *storytelling* and *character*. The energy art embodies speaks through both media and moves across, from one to another artistic form, sometimes in the work of individuals who have practised in both forms. Picasso and Turner were both poets of real interest. William Blake was not only a great poet but a major artist. Nobel laureate Derek Walcott's evocation of the West Indies is vivid in the imagery not only of his poems but also of his paintings. And perhaps the most famous of all artist-poets would be Michelangelo.

There is more to this than mere illustration: Victorian illustrated novels and rich pictorial reference books are a distinct genre, as are contemporary graphic novels with their antecedents in popular comic books. In France, graphic novels are treated seriously as artistic productions whereas in Britain they are more often objects of condescension. The combined visual and literary impact in all these works has to be carefully balanced by their creators. And this balance of components might prompt consideration of television or film adaptations of literary classics, where particularly striking visual images have been grafted onto the author's words in ways that remain memorable: for example, the BBC versions of Lewis Grassic Gibbon's novels and stories, David Lean's film of Dickens's *Great Expectations* or Roman Polanski's of Hardy's *Tess*. But these are prose examples and perhaps one of the dangers of the twenty-first century in the west is the extent to which visual impression is overwhelming: the strafing commercialism of advertising insists on it. So is it intrinsically more difficult for poetry and visual arts to have a dialogue? The subtlety of Margaret Tait's film-portrait of Hugh MacDiarmid suggests that it may be, though the rewards are great.

Perhaps the most intimate modern example of a commerce between the arts of painting and poetry is to be found in the work of the great American poet Ezra Pound, who valuably emphasised the work of the orientalist Ernest Fenollosa and his notes for an essay entitled *The Chinese Written Character as a Medium for Poetry*. Fenollosa's idea, which Pound made much of, was essentially that the Chinese written character was a visual image, a representative drawing, an ideogram, and that the linguistic and literary meaning that followed from it could be conveyed pictorially and quickly. There was no time for abstraction in this language. As Pound elaborated on this theme, the literary movement known as 'Imagism' was given the green light and Pound himself supplied some of its most memorable poetic examples. Pound's friend, the sculptor Henri Gaudier-Brzeska (who was the subject of a biographical study by H.S. Ede and a fine film by Ken Russell, both called *Savage Messiah*), claimed to be able to 'read' Chinese by looking at the characters pictorially. In early twenty-first century China, however, the radical literary revolutions of Pound's modernist poetics were very foreign to the establishment view of art. Over the entrance to the Forbidden Palace in Beijing hangs a gigantic portrait of Chairman Mao. Every year a young Chinese artist is invited – it is considered a great privilege – to paint a new portrait to replace the old one. But the new one must be identical in every respect. There is no place for innovation. In this respect, Chinese artistic tradition is based on the belief that the artist must do the same thing as has been done before, but better. The contrast with western art is clear: at least since Romanticism, western art has glorified self-expression, individualism, the making of something new, and the more shockingly so, the better. In the western world in the twenty-first century, the shock of the new is a familiar modernist aesthetic. And yet, even if we still refer to the international cultural movement which crystallised this aesthetic from the 1890s to the 1930s as 'The Modern', perhaps it is possible to describe a new balance in the post-'Postmodern' twenty-first century. Edwin Morgan is the poet who, in an international arena, most clearly and lucidly carries us forward into this new world.

Morgan belongs to two important groups or small constellations of major poets – one comprising his generation of Scottish poets, who all began publishing important works after World War II. Each wrote fluently in at least one of the indigenous Scottish languages – Gaelic, Scots and English – and each was profoundly connected to a particular geographical area of Scotland. Sorley MacLean, Norman MacCaig, Iain Crichton Smith, George Mackay Brown, Sydney Goodsir Smith and Robert Garioch were all connected also by friendship or acquaintance with Hugh MacDiarmid (1892–1978), who literally came out of the nineteenth century and wrote his most revolutionary work in the 1920s, concurrently with Eliot and Joyce. Edwin Morgan is the last survivor of this astonishing generation of Scotsmen and, in latter years, the most widely-read and best-loved Scottish poet since Robert Burns. But he should also be seen in the company of poets writing in English in an international context: Seamus Heaney, Derek Walcott, Les Murray, Adrienne Rich – poets whose global provenance Morgan also inhabits easefully.

One characteristic of all these poets was that their vision encompassed more than their own art. Music, painting, different kinds of artistic expression were of vital and practising concern to many. This was part of their comprehensive vision of society as a whole. Morgan's poetry exemplifies this: let's take one example. The final poem in Morgan's sequence of responses to Scotland's favourite paintings, *Flood Tide*, relates to Joan Eardley's seascape and the wild natural ethos of Scotland's east coast. But Eardley is also significant as an artist working with people in Glasgow's tenements and slums, painting portraits and buildings, cityscapes and group-portraits in the 1940s and 1950s. One small painting (just over six inches by just under nine inches) was bought by Morgan in the early 1960s and is the subject of a much earlier poem, *To Joan Eardley*.

When, in his 80s, Morgan left his home at 19 Whittinghame Court, near Anniesland in Glasgow's West End, and moved to a nursing home to be looked after, he donated his collection of paintings to the Hunterian Art Gallery at Glasgow University, but he held on to a small number of works to keep by him, and this Eardley was amongst them. He took it with him after that nursing home closed and he went to live in another one, Clarence Court, again in Glasgow's West End. It remains an important painting for him, one of his very few most essential possessions.

To Joan Eardley

Pale yellow letters
humbly straggling across
the once brilliant red
of a broken shop-face
CONFECTIO
and a blur of children

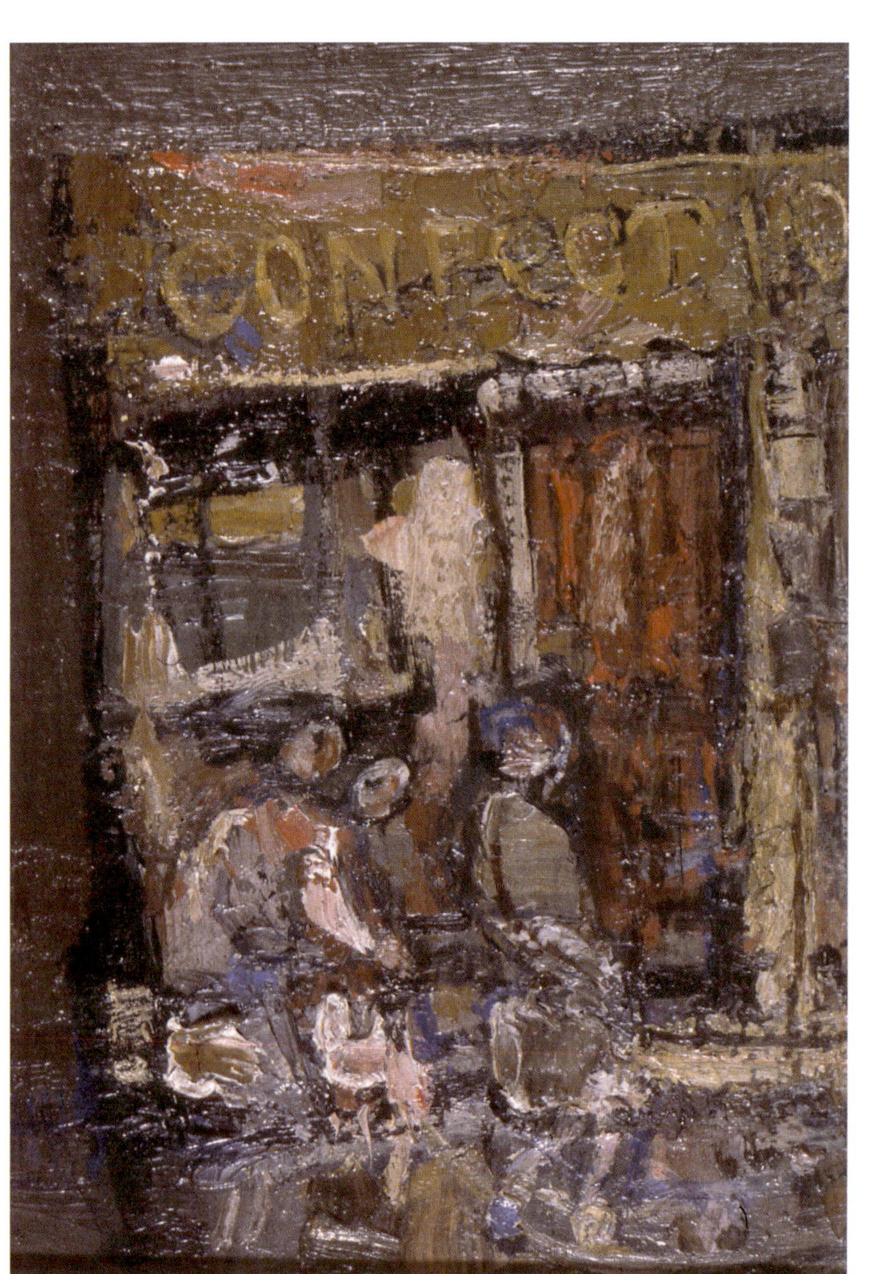

at their games, passing,
gazing as they pass
at the blur of sweets
in the dingy, cosy
Rottenrow window –
an Eardley on my wall.
Such rags and streaks
that master us! –
that fix what the pick
and bulldozer have crumbled
to a dingier dust,
the living blur
fiercely guarding
energy that has vanished,
cries filling still
the unechoing close!
I wandered by the rubble
and the houses left standing
kept a chill, dying life
in their islands of stone.
no window opened
as the coal cart rolled
and the coalman's call
fell coldly to the ground.
But the shrill children
jump on my wall.

Look at this poem closely for a moment. The first eleven lines describe the painting and the twelfth discloses what it is. The poem is dated April 1962 and was published by Edinburgh University Press in Morgan's first substantial collection *The Second Life* in 1968, and even today, the reader has to work at the inferences and references to the specific Glasgow location (Rottenrow – the name itself is redolent of the squalor of slum-life) and the era in which the tenements were being demolished in the early 1960s, before there were new flats and houses replacing them.

The next ten lines (lines 13–22) are an exclamation. The tone is rhapsodic and meditative. The exclamation mark acknowledging the mastering power of 'rags and streaks' in art and life is followed by a long dash as the sentence runs forward, with the repetition of 'that' and the emphasis on 'the living blur' (the word 'blur' recurs to describe the children (in line 6), the sweets in the shop-window (line 9) and then as a noun in its own right (in line 18). The actual pick and bulldozer have broken down the buildings and the energy that animated the children in that actual place has 'vanished' – but at the centre of Morgan's poem is this exclamation of pleasure in the way the painting continues its work of 'fiercely guarding' that energy. The painting is a protection and an embodiment in its evocation, of that energy.

The next eight lines (lines 23–30) present the poet, or his persona, taking a walk among the ruins and rubble of the buildings depicted in the painting. The houses left undemolished are silent. A coalman passes with his cart and the assonance (the repeated 'oh' sound in 'stone', 'coal', 'coalman's' and 'coldly') and the alliteration (of the hard 'c' and lingering 'l' sounds) emphasise the solitary sound of his cry in the unanswering air.

Then the final two lines (lines 31–32) deliver Morgan's ultimate assertion and affirmation of the value of art, its permanent sense of preserving the example those energies set. The 'shrill children' are still there, still shouting, acting, living, as they 'jump on my wall'. It's an appropriate poem to complement the one which closes the present book, where Morgan focuses on Eardley's other main subject beside the children of the city: the sea.

Such things remind us, without embarrassment or sentimentalisation, of elemental realities which do indeed 'master us'. Going into a good art gallery, experiencing the stillness and living vibration in the air when people are seeing things, allows us to acknowledge quietly the truth in Turner's alleged last words, that vatic exclamation, 'The sun is God!' or to recollect the intense consolation and challenge of Wallace Stevens's great poem, 'Waving Adieu, Adieu, Adieu' which begins:

> That would be waving and that would be crying,
> Crying and shouting and meaning farewell,
> Farewell in the eyes and farewell at the centre,
> Just to stand still without moving a hand.

The poem goes on to evoke the act of 'beholding' – to be 'one's singular self' and 'turn / To the ever-jubilant weather':

> What is there here but weather, what spirit
> Have I except it comes from the sun?

Morgan, like Stevens, takes special pleasure in the weather of his native place. He was appointed to the position of first-ever National Poet of Scotland (or 'Scots Makar') on 16 February 2004, at the age of 83. Many people reading the news or watching it on television took pleasure in the fact that at last Scotland could make a decidedly public statement about the central importance of poetry and the arts in this way. It was not always so. Yet the relation of writers and art in modern Scotland is rich in curiosity: famously, Alasdair Gray, John Byrne and Liz Lochhead all studied at the Glasgow School of Art before they became important writers in Scotland. Hugh MacDiarmid collaborated with the great lyric abstract painter William Johnstone on a book of poems and lithographs in the 1970s, and in the 1930s he produced a small group of poems addressing the nature of Johnstone's art. Among Edwin Morgan's contemporaries, Norman MacCaig, George Bruce and Duncan Glen have all produced poems in response to, or as accompaniments to, particular paintings. And there are correspondences in other countries. From Ireland, Paul Durcan and from Australia, Les Murray, have each produced books of poems to 'accompany' reproductions of paintings from their respective national collections.

The sequence of poems in this book, however, is neither merely descriptive of the paintings they accompany, nor independent of them. Nor docs it address a single artist or theory. They are published in the sequence Morgan himself arranged and connect with each other. They are spirited, enquiring, possessed of what Marshall Walker once characterised as a key quality in Morgan's mind: 'the intrinsic optimism of curiosity'. They are often witty and funny, or surprising (look for the cross-reference between James McIntosh Patrick's window-view and Cadell's orange blind), but they are also critical of the glamour and misleading glitter which surfaces can convey (Sargent's Lady Agnew is a 'society sitter' painted by a 'society painter' while the *Man in Armour* stands rather glossily over the realities of 'the death of men' and although Morgan admits that Rembrandt is a great painter, for the poet this painting is much more glitz than insight). They are also, as you read and re-read them and let them sink in, increasingly moving, from the religious speculation in response to Dalí's painting of the crucifixion, where light arrives 'from where we cannot see' – another dimension, perhaps, another time – to the final poem about Joan Eardley, who rejected the 'glitter of salons' in favour of the free salt wind and clifftop by the sea, where spray and the gale might carry grass and clover to be caught in the paint, in the painting itself, and become the art, while the artist, like the poet, or any of us looking and reading, move 'beyond the sun'. It is worth noting that the facsimile reproduction of Morgan's manuscript shows that the last line of this last poem was simply that phrase, and subsequently the poet added the preceding phrase, 'As she is now'.

Morgan's poems take part in a curious dialogue, or rather, an open conversation arising from the past but directed towards the future, a conversation with different listeners and viewers: with the paintings themselves (both as material artefacts and in terms of what they depict), with the artists who painted them, with the readers of *The Herald* who voted for them, and so with an extending constituency who will see them and think a little more about what Morgan has to say about all these things, and what his poems imply about the openness and value of that conversation and the life all art embodies.

Professor Alan Riach
HEAD OF THE DEPARTMENT OF SCOTTISH LITERATURE
UNIVERSITY OF GLASGOW

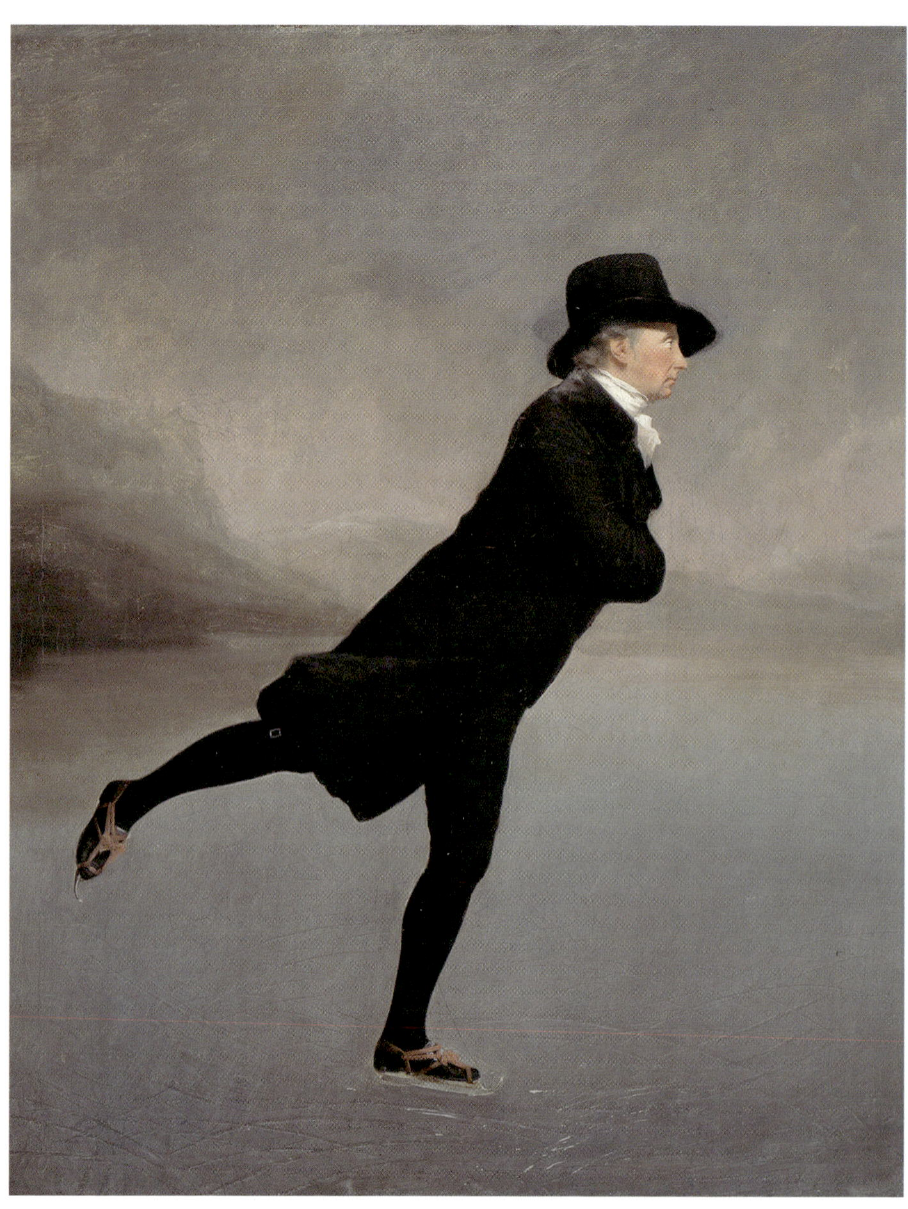

The Reverend Robert Walker Skating on Duddingston Loch

Sir Henry Raeburn

The skating minister is well balanced
And knows it. Something distinctly smug
Keeps those arms in place. Wouldn't it be good
If the god of thaws pulled that icy rug
From under him, to remind his next sermon
What it is that goeth before a fall.
He shivers before the fire
Hunched in his wife's mocking shawl –
Not the thing at all!

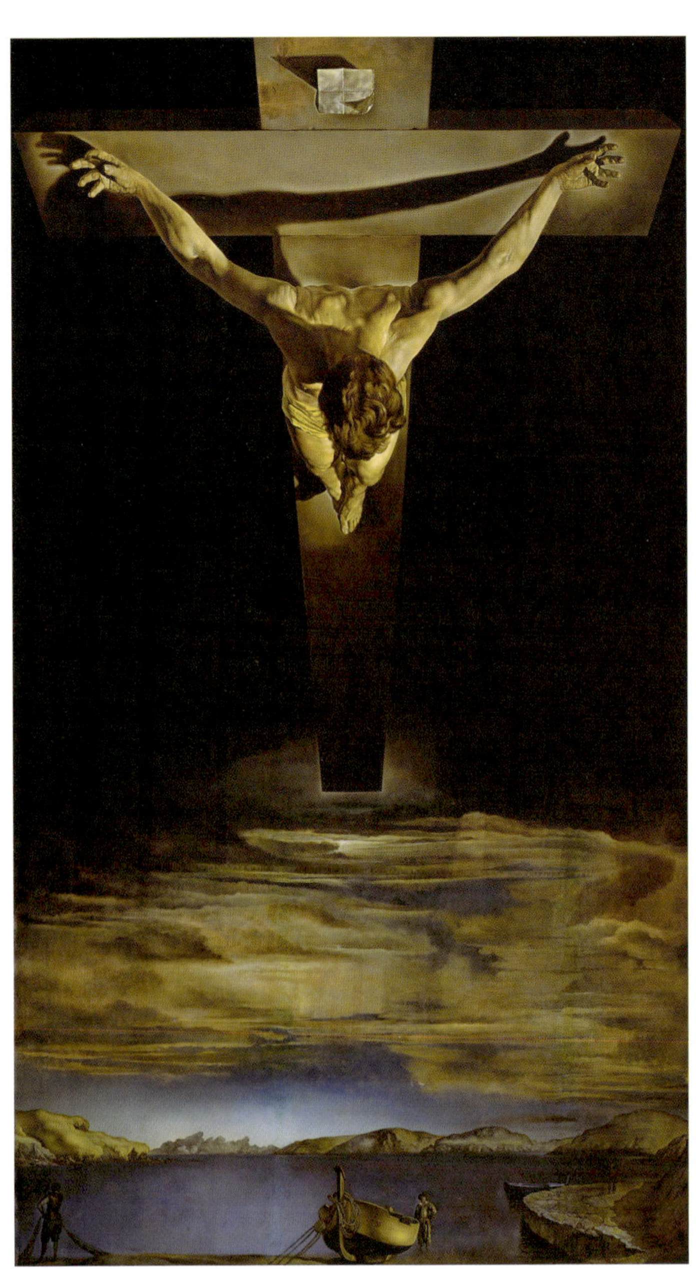

Christ of St John of the Cross

Salvador Dalí

It is not of this world, and yet it is,
And that is how it should be.
Strong light hits the back and the arms
Coming from where we cannot see,
Ought not to see, another dimension
For another time. At this time, we
Share the life of bay and boat
With simply painted fishermen
Who would give no Amen
Even if clouds both apocalyptic and real
Made them look up and feel
What they had to feel
Of shattering amazement, fear,
Protection, and a wash of glory.
Was it an end coming near?
Was it a beginning coming near?
What happened to the thorns and blood and sweat?
What happened to the hands like claws the whipcord muscles?
Has the artist never seen Grünewald?
'I have to tell you John of the Cross called,
Said to remind you light and death once met.'

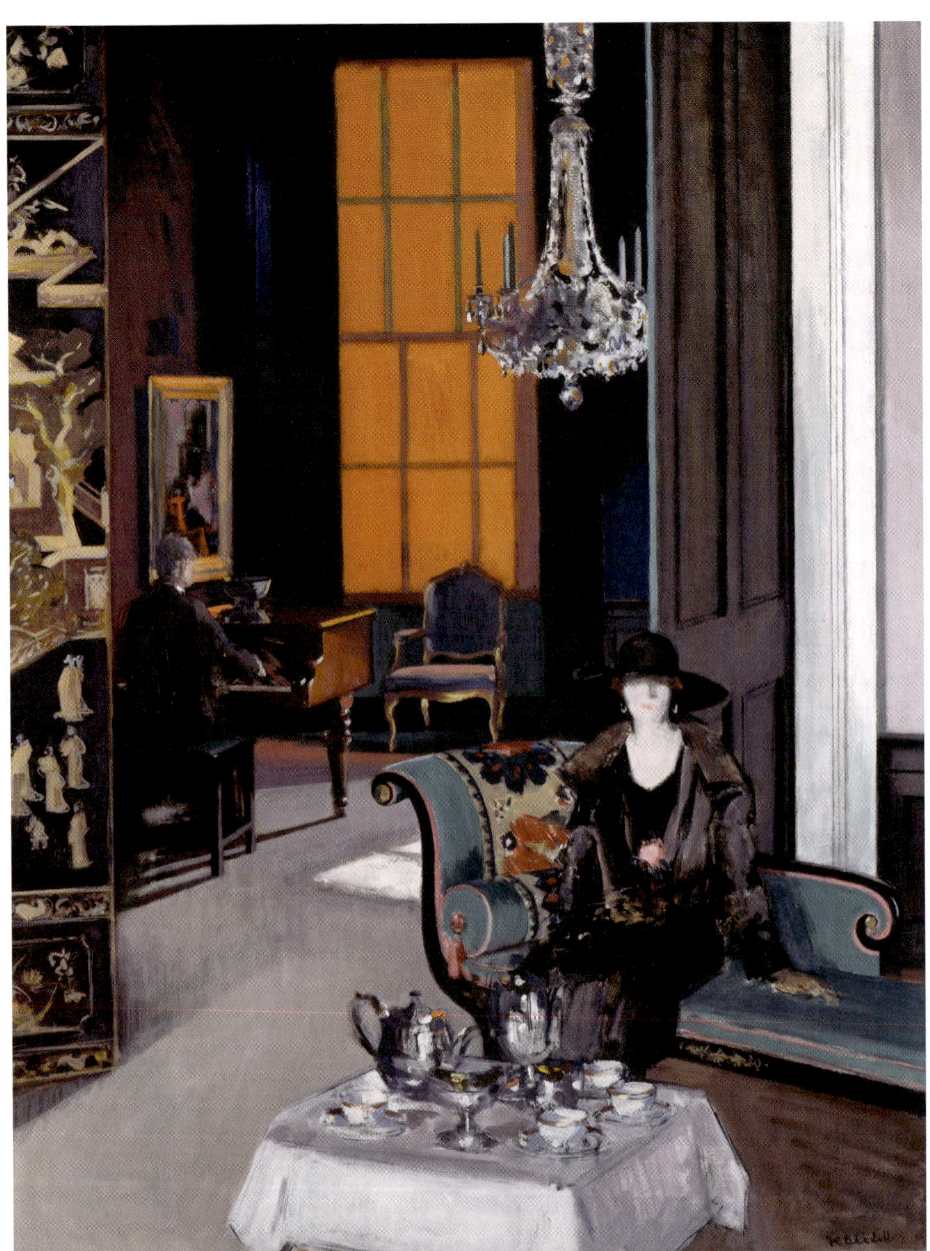

The Orange Blind

F.C.B. Cadell

I was a gawky seven-year-old
When this elegant picture was painted.
High verticals and a chandelier
Tell us it was no sheepfold,
And the dash of orange
Gives it no peer.
King Charles's 'Look after poor Nell!'
Is oranges as well –
Best in town! And the glorious sun,
As orange as they come.
Beats the orange and the mandrill's bum.

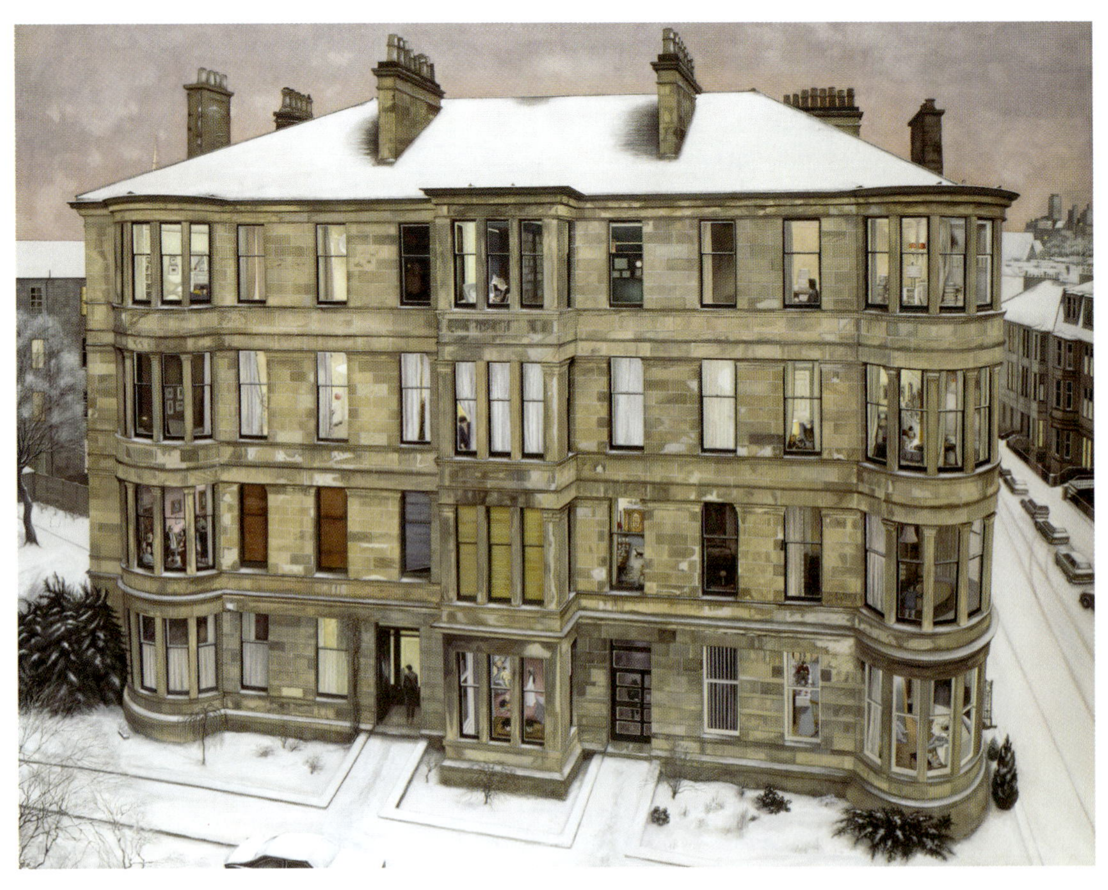

Windows in the West

Avril Paton

Turn the kaleidoscope and the seventy-eyed creature
Stretches, yawns, shakes the roof snow
Off its back in clumsy dollops, gets a glow
Going, cries of 'It's freezing!' (not really, just a feature
Of tenement winter), puts some coffee on, come on –
How can a single one be a multiple seventy –
I don't know, but I know I like the mystery –
Breathe out, breathe in, never in unison –
'When did you get in last night?' – 'Where the hell
Did you put my razor?' – 'Dog has started
To chew things up again' – 'Well, well,
You were going to give it a bone, that's your department' –
'That was never what art meant,
Pictures falling off the wall, everyone has a –'
'Don't throw it away. I might need it' –
'You'll never write a line if you don't heed it
When I tell you there's enough life,
Enough strife
In this old sandstone block
To turn *Anna Karenina* and *The Great Gatsby*
Into one noble undefeated cry
Which is the single tenement sigh
Any time, anywhere.
Turn up the heat,
A new day's always sweet.'
'Coffee up.'
'My god another cracked cup.'

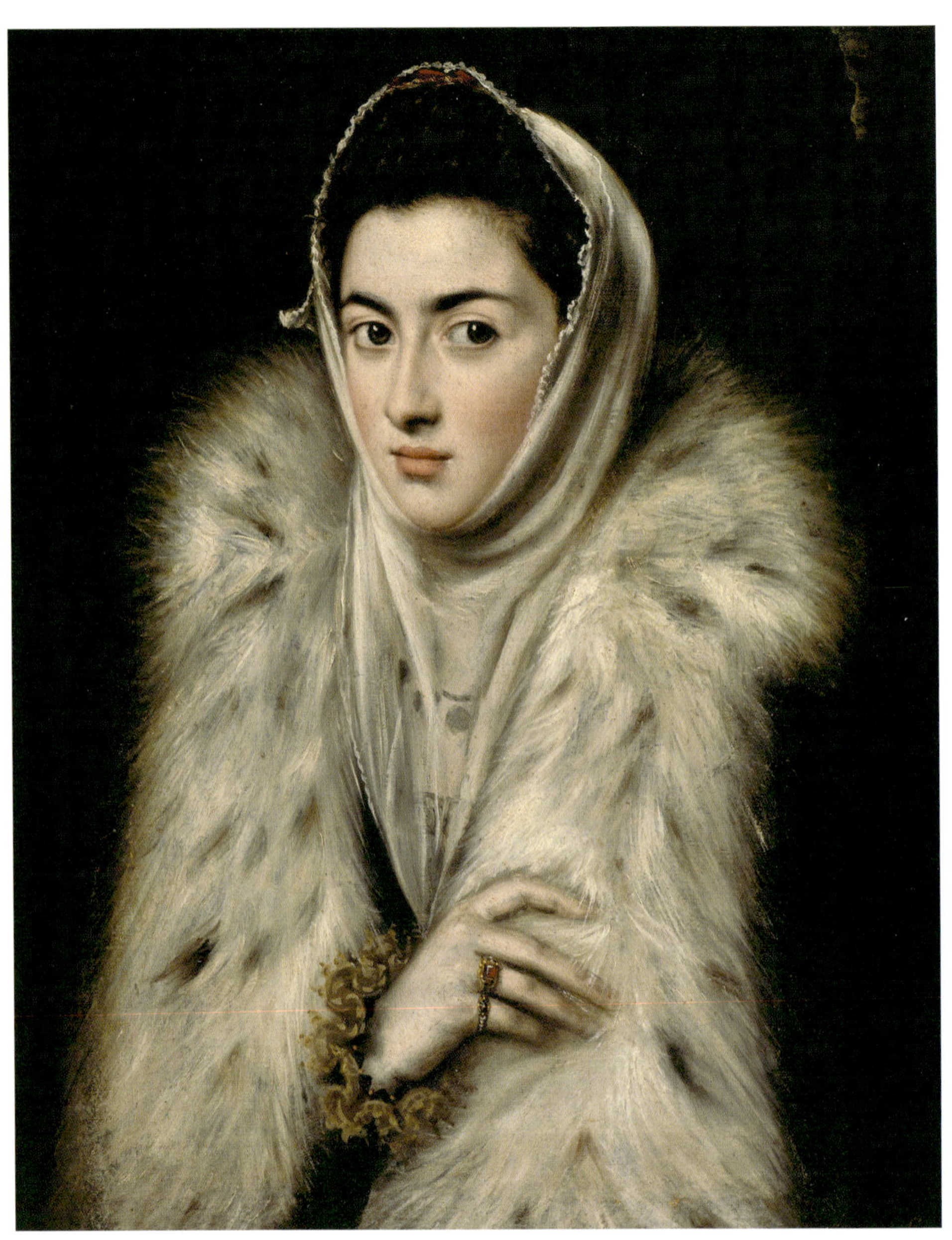

Lady in a Fur Wrap

El Greco

The fur will be real, not *faux*,
But don't let that spoil the delight
With which you watch her stroke it,
So do not mock it.
It was the habit of the time to show
A little ermine if you could afford it
And then proceed to lord it
Over your girlfriends, not hiding your rings,
Arranging your headscarf to be both modest and eye-catching.
The portrait is called *A Lady* and that is enough
For anyone. Whoever she was,
She gives the world an unforgettable glance
From which we don't advance
With names. Let the great Greek who painted her
Keep his secret as long as he will.

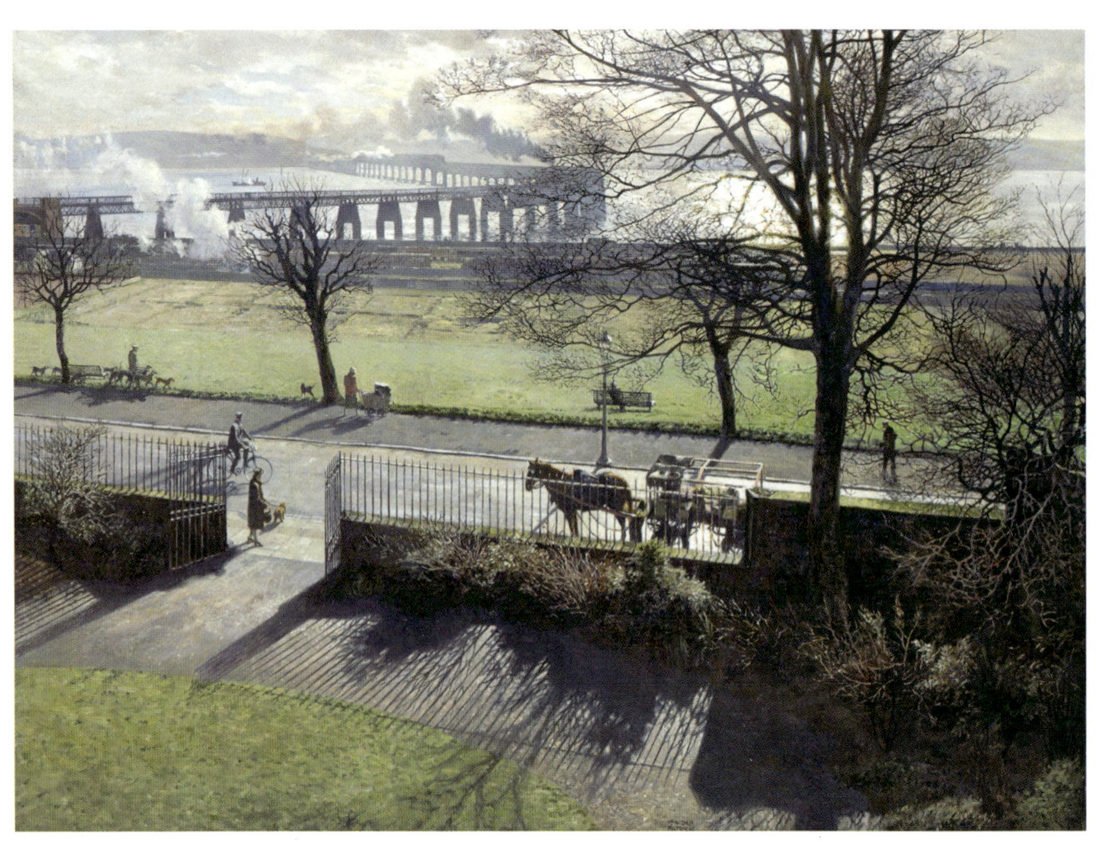

The Tay Bridge from my Studio Window

James McIntosh Patrick

A very lucky photograph might catch such light and shade
But anyone who sees it
Knows it has been made,
Made beautiful, made a little strange,
With no lens to freeze it,
Freeze the placing of components
For once not needed, or scarcely so,
In a moment of bare trees and madly curving bridge
To catch the eye. A familiar scene
Centres on the patience of a horse
With drooping head and on the criss-cross
Of sunlight and shadow filtered by the railings.
If you see any failings
(And you may not), you could blame
The perfection of nature when it chimes
With a man's mood of harmony and peace
And you find
You miss the orange blind.

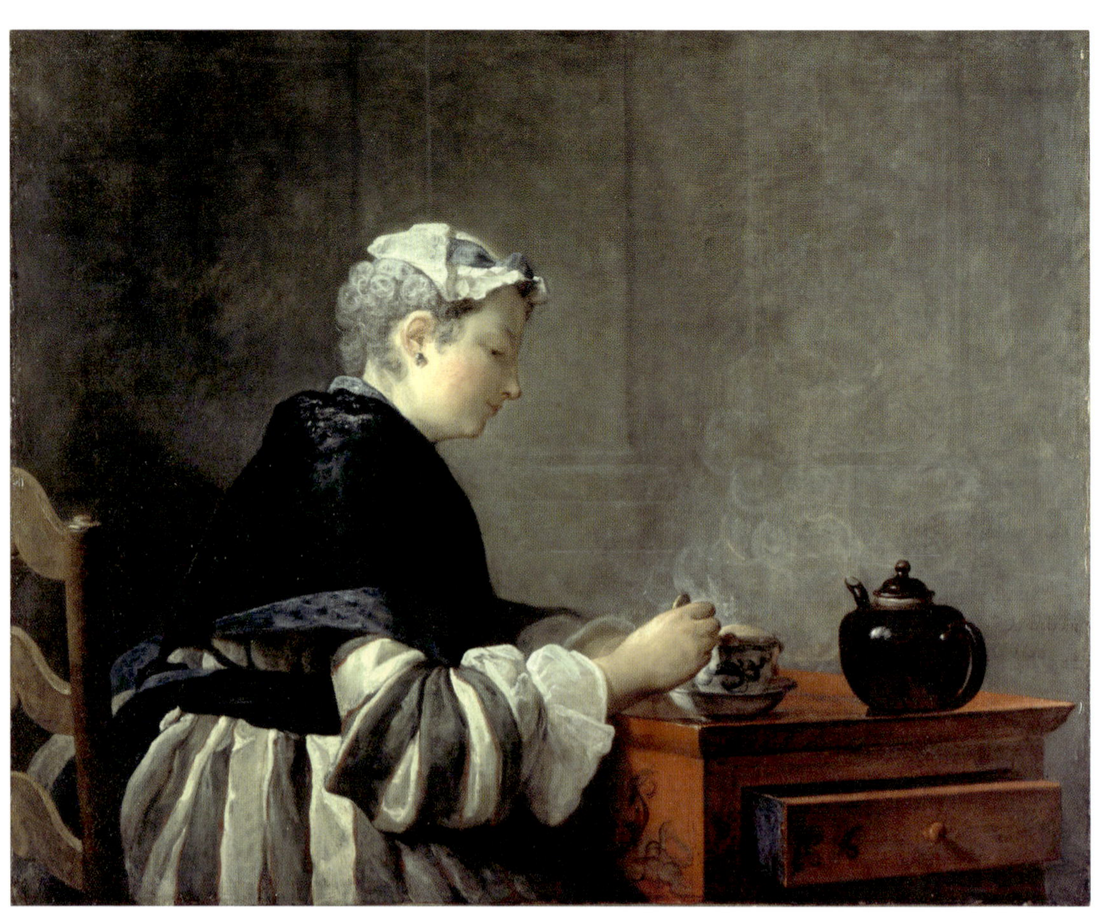

Lady Taking Tea

Jean-Simeon Chardin

Thank you thank you but we have seen too many lily-white Annunciations.
We could flock-paper a whole library room with sad Stabat Maters.
We could tapestry a flash-flood parlour with triumphant Assumptions.
Can you imagine the relief, the delight, the quiet ovation
Time has engineered out of simplicity?
And do not think she had brought out her silver tea-service:
Everything was natural, in use, well made, you can see
She is not entertaining, but taking a break from her chores,
No tablecloth, but nothing scruffy or sloppy,
Her striped skirt shows she keeps up appearances,
Would no doubt turn the radio on,
An artist's wife as we think she was,
Not one for dances or romances,
She dreams a moment, staring into the future
Where, if she knew it, great art can be
An ordinary woman sipping tea.

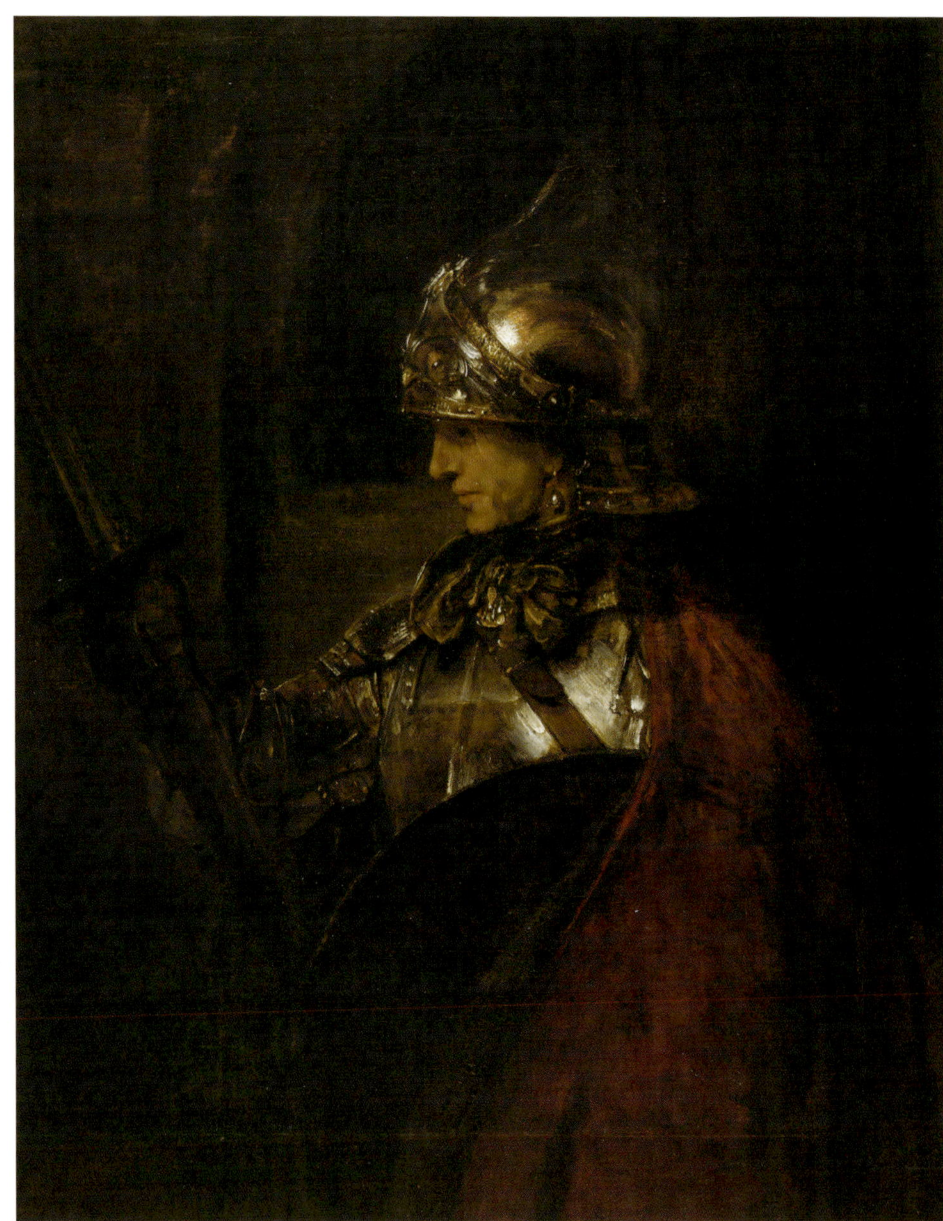

Man in Armour

Rembrandt

No warrior here.
This is a man who has put on some armour
In the cause of art. No enemy is near,
The helmet is well burnished and no doubt,
If tapped, gives off a musical note.
It would certainly not
Smudge hand or glove with caked or dusty blood.
If the man is faintly smiling, that would fit.
Rembrandt, man, everyone will love it.

Bring back your son, yourself, the woman at her bath,
And we'll use words like masterpiece again,
A cupboard is the best place for jingle-jangle.
Oh it's well done: the head looms out of darkness
With all the accoutrements bar pain,
You are great; even a loss from you's a gain.
But do not trivialize the death of men.

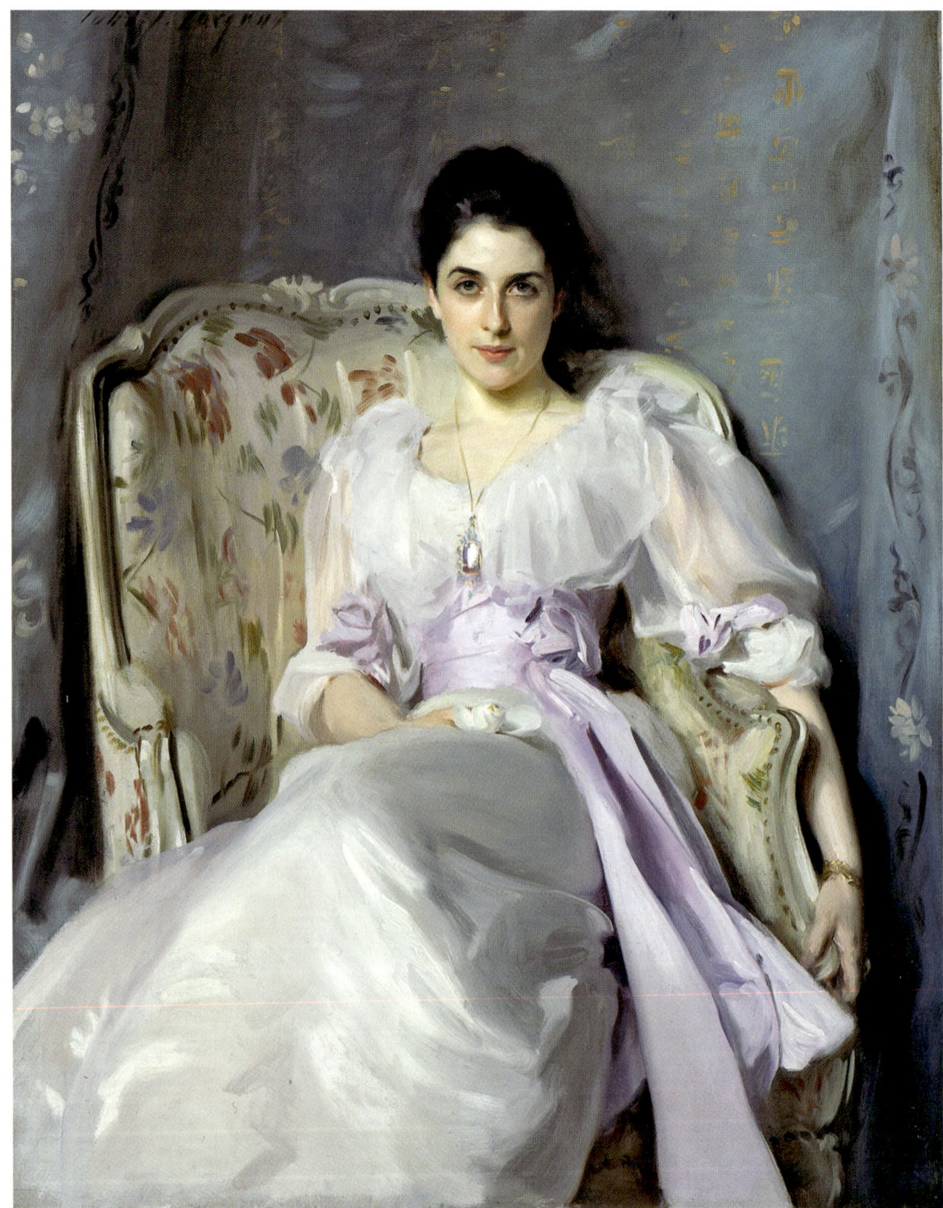

Lady Agnew of Lochnaw

J.S. Sargent

A woman of character looks straight at us.
Character more than beauty shall we say? –
But just because of that, a classic portrait
That tells us she was worth a brush or two.
Dark hair and light loose dress show without fuss
The nature of an aristocracy
That has not gone to seed, and what comes through
Is *fin de siècle* lacking the decadence
Some would miss. 'Make me glamorous.'
'But you are glamorous, my dear.'
'What is art for, except to improve on nature?'
'To be blunt, if you have a good feature
I shall not miss it out. But if you had such a splendid nose
You wanted it more than life size, or wanted two,
I'd have to pass you over to Picasso.
Come on now, we are what we are,
Society painter, society sitter.
Scrub thoughts of Cleopatra on her litter.'

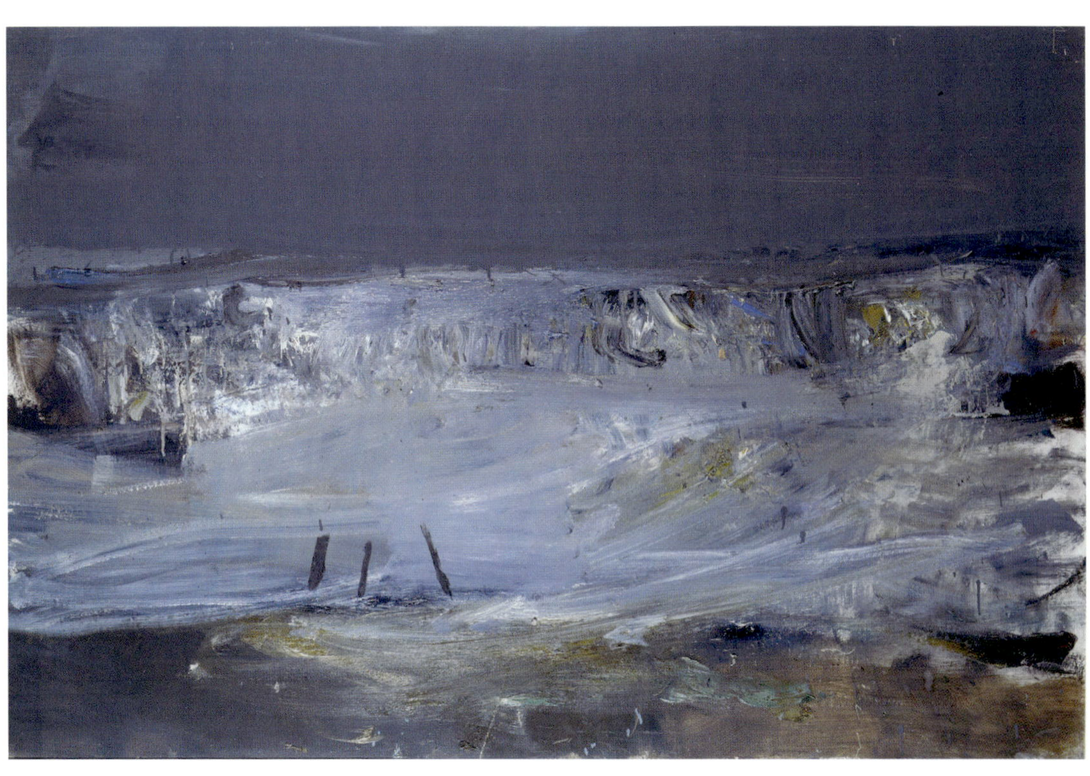

Flood Tide

Joan Eardley

Lonely people are drawn to the sea.
Not for this artist the surge and glitter of salons,
Clutch of a sherry or making polite conversation.
See her when she is free: –
Striding into the salty bluster of a cliff-top
In her paint-splashed corduroys,
Humming as she recalls the wild shy boys
She sketched in the city, allowing nature's nations
Of grasses and wild shy flowers to stick
To the canvas they were blown against
By the mighty Catterline wind –
All becomes art, and as if it was incensed
By the painter's brush the sea growls up
In a white flood.
The artist's cup
Is overflowing with what she dares
To think is joy, caught unawares
As if on the wing. A solitary clover,
Unable to read WET PAINT, rolls over
Once, twice, and then it's fixed,
Part of a field more human than the one
That took the gale and is now
As she is, beyond the sun.

2/

(2) JOAN EARDLEY: FLOOD-TIDE

Lonely people are drawn to the sea.
Not for this artist the surge and glitter of salons,
Clutching a sherry and making polite conversation.
See her when she is free! —
Striding over the salty bluster of a cliff-top
In her paint-splashed corduroys,
Humming as she recalls the wild shy boys
She sketched in the city, allowing nature's oblations
Of grasses and wild shy flowers to stick
To the canvas they were blown against
By the mighty Catterline wind —
All becomes art, and as if it was incensed
By the painter's brush the sea growls up
Into a white flood. [illegible]
The artist's cup
Is overflowing with what she dares
To think is joy, caught unawares
As if on the wing. A solitary clover,
Unable to resist WET PAINT, rolls over
Once, twice, and then it's stuck,
Part of a field more human than the one
That took the gale and is now
As she is, Beyond the sun.

23

Time has engraved out of simplicity?

(4) JEAN-SIMEON: LADY TAKING TEA

Thank you thank you but we have seen too many lily-white Annunciations.
We could flock-paper a whole living room with sad Stabat Maters.
We could tapestry a [illegible] parlour with triumphant Assumptions.
You can imagine the relief, the delight, the quiet ovation
And do not think she had brought out her silver tea-service:
Everything was natural, [illegible] in use, well made, you can see
She is not entertaining but taking a break from her chores,
No tablecloth, nothing scruffy or sloppy,
Her striped dress shows she keeps up appearances,
Would no doubt stroll the road in,
An artist's wife as we think she was,
Not one for dances or romances,
She dreams a moment, staring into the future
Where, if she knew it, great art can be
An ordinary woman sipping tea.

16

[illegible]

AFTERWORD

NOW YOU'RE READING THIS afterword, you, like me, will have had the pleasure first of all of looking, feasting your eyes; then an enjoyable and lively dialogue between these ten very popular and familiar paintings and Scotland's greatest, most popular poet, Edwin Morgan. As well as Lesley Duncan's delighted account of the surprise she got one morning in her mail at *The Herald*, and a sparkling but penetrating essay illuminating the relationship between poetry and painting by Alan Riach, who – like Eddie before him – is also an academic, but first and foremost a poet.

My favourite moment in that essay – oh, apart from the in-full quoting of Morgan's great poem *To Joan Eardley* (the city Eardley, the Townhead Eardley, his own) – is when Alan shares Marshall Walker's aperçu that a key quality of Morgan's mind is 'the intrinsic optimism of curiosity'.

For Morgan is quite simply interested in everything. Always. Looking up now at the spread of his books on my shelves I see leap out at me titles like (my favourite) *From Glasgow to Saturn* and a book of essays entitled *Nothing Not Giving Messages*. Doesn't that say it all? Perhaps not surprising that seeing the results of a Top Ten Favourite Paintings poll in Scotland's biggest daily paper he was not one to fulminate snootily against such lists as 'dumbing down' or 'irrelevant' (or yawning and calling the results 'predictable') but was fascinated by why these paintings had been chosen by us, what this says, as well as by the images which endure.

So he swiftly, deftly, instantly, like an artist with his most thumbnail sketchbook – just look at the draft page, the life in that! the upward inflections of the lines, the relatively few re-orderings and scratchings out – put down in a spare few lines his first, or his most rapidly retrieved, responses.

What we get here is as intimate as something overheard. He takes these paintings personally. So puts himself in the picture, telling us, telling himself, that he was 'a gawky seven-year-old' when Cadell's *Orange Blind*, that gorgeous Glasgow icon, was painted. He sees through Raeburn's famous skating minister with a delicate irony which for all its humour is by no means entirely affectionate, concentrating on the Reverend Walker himself in a different picture all of Morgan's own (and word-limned), and doesn't for a moment dwell upon Raeburn and whether he painted it or not.

Other times it's the artist in the art he celebrates – as in his wee row to Rembrandt, or his valediction of El Greco's reticence and mystery, or his profound empathy with Eardley, with the freedom of art when you're doing it, even beaten up by the bluster on dangerous cliffs in heavy weather, 'allowing nature's nations / Of grasses and wild shy flowers to stick'.

Reading between the lines we know which of these paintings Morgan really loves. We share, for instance, in his delight in the decorum of the Chardin and the quotidian marvel that '...great art can be / An ordinary woman taking tea'. In the art which Morgan loves – and he loves all art which celebrates life – there is the moment, *that moment in time*, captured but still perfectly free, and therefore the great mystery of all that is before, after, beyond it.

Listening to this conversation between ten paintings and a man you'll have been chiming in with comments and arguments of your own. Though what you chipped in with isn't here recorded.

I've scribbled down in my notebook a rough collage of few fragments filched from this book. Under 'Such rags and streaks that master us' (that long beloved quote from the earlier Eardley poem) come, scattergun, random, '. . .the glorious sun, / As orange as they come. / Beats the orange and the mandrill's bum' . . . 'the shrill children / jump on my wall' . . . 'the god of thaws'. . . and the image of the tenement as a creature shrugging 'the roof snow / Off its back in clumsy dollops' . . . 'At this time, we / Share the life of bay and boat' and 'beyond the sun'.

Ah. Beyond the sun.

Liz Lochhead

POET LAUREATE OF GLASGOW

Luath Press Limited

committed to publishing well written books worth reading

LUATH PRESS takes its name from Robert Burns, whose little collie Luath (*Gael.*, swift or nimble) tripped up Jean Armour at a wedding and gave him the chance to speak to the woman who was to be his wife and the abiding love of his life. Burns called one of 'The Twa Dogs' Luath after Cuchullin's hunting dog in Ossian's *Fingal*. Luath Press was established in 1981 in the heart of Burns country, and now resides a few steps up the road from Burns' first lodgings on Edinburgh's Royal Mile.

Luath offers you distinctive writing with a hint of unexpected pleasures.

Most bookshops in the UK, the US, Canada, Australia, New Zealand and parts of Europe either carry our books in stock or can order them for you. To order direct from us, please send a £sterling cheque, postal order, international money order or your credit card details (number, address of cardholder and expiry date) to us at the address below. Please add post and packing as follows: UK – £1.00 per delivery address; overseas surface mail – £2.50 per delivery address; overseas airmail – £3.50 for the first book to each delivery address, plus £1.00 for each additional book by airmail to the same address. If your order is a gift, we will happily enclose your card or message at no extra charge.

ILLUSTRATION: IAN KELLAS

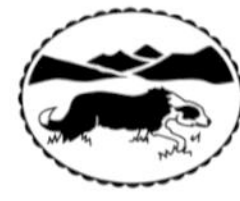

Luath Press Limited
543/2 Castlehill
The Royal Mile
Edinburgh EH1 2ND
Scotland
Telephone: 0131 225 4326 (24 hours)
Fax: 0131 225 4324
email: sales@luath.co.uk
Website: www.luath.co.uk